The Internationalization of BRICS Currencies:
China's Experiences and Cooperation Strategy

Liu Dongmin, Xiao Lisheng, Lu Ting, Xiong Aizong, Zhang Chi

 Paths International Ltd

 中国社会科学出版社
CHINA SOCIAL SCIENCES PRESS

Contents

Abstract: As big emerging economies, BRICS countries have real demand for their currencies internationalization. China started facilitating RMB internationalization after 2008 financial crisis and has made significant achievement since then. RMB internationalization is facing challenge now because the expectation of RMB appreciation has disappeared and capital account has not completely opened yet. Promoting BRICS's currencies internationalization by cooperation among BRICS countries will be of benefit for both RMB internationalization and diversifying the international monetary system. This report gives some proposals for facilitating BRICS currencies internationalization through financial cooperation: promoting the development of local currency bond market, enhancing the local currency financing and investing in BRICS countries, further strengthening the currency swap and direct trade, launching the local currency settlement in commodity trade, piloting the financial infrastructure among BRICS countries with blockchain.

Keywords: BRICS, RMB internationalzation, local currency bond market, blockchain

The Chinese government has begun to gradually promote RMB internationalization since the 2008 global financial crisis. The pressing need for the reform of the international monetary system, the steady growth of the Chinese economy, the government's support and the RMB appreciation expectation over the past several years have worked together to propel RMB internationalization. Inclusion of RMB into SDR currency basket in October 2016 highlighted the international community's recognition of the achievement of RMB internationalization.

RMB internationalization faces many challenges today as the country is yet to achieve full capital account convertibility and RMB depreciation expectation is rising. Strengthening cooperation among BRICS countries to promote internationalization of their currencies is not only of vital importance for RMB internationalization but also a major step to propel diversified development of the international monetary system. ①

①　The Institute of World Economics and Politics collaborates with other five think tanks from BRICS countries to implement the joint research " Wider usage of national currencies in international settlements, particularly among the BRICS". This report is the China's report of the joint research which is sponsored by International Politics and Financial Security Program.

1 The Background and Goal of China's Efforts to Promote RMB Internationalization

The Chinese government has promoted RMB internationalization against such a background that, on the one hand, the 2008 global financial crisis has made the international community keenly aware of the inherent instability of the international monetary system with the dominance of the US dollar and the urgent need of a diversified international monetary system as the most likely rational choice in the future, which has thus created real external demand for RMB internationalization; on the other hand, the tremendous progress that the Chinese economy has made through reform and opening up over more than three decades has provided the inherent driving force for RMB internationalization.

As early as in the era of the Bretton Woods system, US

scholar Robert Triffin identified the "Triffin Dilemma" that the country, whose currency is made a global reserve currency, must supply the world with an extra supply of its currency through continuous trade deficits to ensure its global liquidity; additionally, continuous trade deficits will lead to devaluation of its currency to weaken other countries' willingness to withhold it. The Triffin Dilemma still exists in the Jamaica system established after the collapse of the Bretton Woods system because the US dollar remains to be the dominant currency of the international monetary system. Some scholars had insisted before 2008 that the United States could afford long-term trade deficits because the return on its overseas investment would exceed the cost of its overseas financing. However, the 2008 global financial crisis has awakened the international community to the inherent instability of the dollar-led international monetary system. The financial crisis broke out because the US mode of low saving, high consumption and high debt built on the dominance of the dollar had become unsustainable. Besides, it was right because of the central role of the dollar in the international monetary system that the US sub-prime crisis had evolved so rapidly into a serious global financial crisis. In view of global financial stability, it is necessary to either introduce a su-

pranational currency to root out the Triffin Dilemma or realize diversification of the international monetary system to
ease the Triffin Dilemma. In reality, since it is difficult to
introduce a supranational currency in the short and medium
term, a diversified international monetary system has become the most feasible choice.

Based on this understanding, the Chinese government
has begun to promote RMB internationalization since the
global financial crisis, aiming to set up a diversified international monetary system to advance global financial stability and enhance China's financial robustness and competitiveness.

2 Policy Implementation and Progress of RMB Internationalization

1. Encourage Enterprises to use RMB Settlement in Cross-border Trade and Investment

In December 2008, China's State Council decided to carry out pilot program on RMB settlement in trade in goods between Guangdong, the Yangtze River Delta and Hong Kong, Macao and between Guangxi, Yunnan and ASEAN. In April 2009, the State Council decided to carry out pilot program on RMB settlement in cross-border trade in Shanghai and Guangdong's Guangzhou, Shenzhen, Zhuhai and Dongguan. In June 2010, People's Bank of China, Ministry of Finance, Ministry of Commerce, General Administration of Customs, State Administration of Taxation and China Banking Regulatory Commission jointly issued "Notice on issues concerning the expansion of pilot program on RMB settlement in cross-border trade", extending the pilot regions from Shanghai and four cities of Guangdong to more than 20 provinces and municipalities including Beijing, Tianjin, Jiangsu, Zhejiang and Fujian. In August 2011, the six government departments jointly issued "Notice on enlarging regions for RMB settlement in cross-border trade", extending the pilot regions to the whole country. It is noteworthy that, instead of putting forward the idea of RMB internationalization, the aim for the central government to advance this pilot program at that time was to help enterprises avoid exchange rate risk and reduce exchange loss. It showed that, during that period, the Chinese government was very cautious about RMB internationalization.

For the purpose of further expanding the use of RMB in cross-border trade and investment and regulating the banks and overseas investors in carrying out settlement for RMB-denominated foreign direct investment, the People's Bank of China had formulated "Administrative Rules on Settlement of RMB-denominated Foreign Direct Investment" on October 14, 2011. This means that overseas investors and the banks can carry out settlement for RMB-denominated foreign direct investment according to the new administrative rules, effectively expanding the cross-border use of RMB and substantially facilitating trade and investment while advancing the progress of RMB internationalization. On June 14, 2012, for the purpose of implementing "Administrative Rules on Settlement of RMB-denominated Foreign Direct Investment", facilitating RMB-denominated foreign direct investment by overseas investors and regulating the banks and financial institutions in carrying out settlement for RMB-denominated foreign direct investment, the People's Bank of China issued "Notice on Specifying Operating Rules on Settlement of RMB-denominated Foreign Direct Investment".

In addition, the People's Bank of China also made joint efforts with other related departments to adopt a series of supportive measures to facilitate the use RMB in cross-border settlement. On July 1, 2009, the People's Bank of China, Ministry of Finance, Ministry of Commerce, General Administration of Customs, State Administration of Taxation and China Banking Regulatory Commission jointly issued "Administrative Rules for the Pilot Program on RMB Settlement of Cross-Border Trade" to regulate the behaviors of pilot enterprises and commercial banks and prevent related business risks so as to promote trade facilitation and ensure smooth implementation of the pilot program on RMB settlement in cross-border trade. To implement "Administrative Rules on Pilot Program of RMB Settlement of Cross-border Trade Transactions", the People's Bank of China and the State Administration of Foreign Exchange had issued in July 2009 respectively "Regulations for Implementing the Administrative Rules on Pilot Program of RMB Settlement of Cross-border Trade Transactions" and "Notice on related issues concerning the declaration and statistics on international receipts and payments in RMB settlement of cross-border trade transactions", so as to facilitate implementation and progress of the use of RMB in cross-border settlement.

RMB cross-border settlement has been accelerating as China's international trade and direct investment keep growing. Currently, RMB cross-border settlement has been expanded to all regions in the country, with no geographic restrictions in overseas markets. According to statistics from People's Bank of China, RMB cross-border settlement has covered more than 210 foreign countries and regions. [1]In term of capital, the amount of actual receipts and payments had both increased year by year before the "August 11" for-

---

① Bank of China: Cross border RMB policy Q&A, http://www. boc. cn/cbservice/cb11/201401/t20140108_2816514. html, Jan. 8, 2014.

eign exchange reform in 2015. After that, the actual receipts of RMB settlement in cross-border trade had begun to decline while the actual payments had fluctuated.

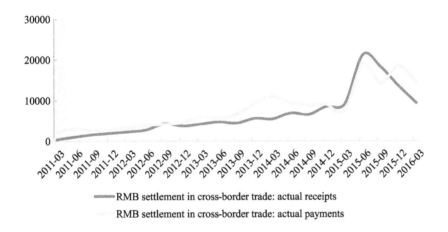

RMB settlement in cross-border trade: actual receipts
RMB settlement in cross-border trade: actual payments

Figure 1   Cross-border flow of RMB fund (**100 million yuan**)

Data source: Wind Database.

The aggregate amount of RMB settlement in cross-border trade has reached 6.47 trillion yuan in the first ten months of 2016 among which trade in goods, standing at 3.46 trillion yuan, accounted for 54% of the total; foreign direct investment, 1.15 trillion yuan, 18%; trade in service and other current accounts, 931.6 billion yuan, 14%; outbound direct investment, 921.1 billion yuan, 14%.

To support implementation of RMB cross-border settlement, China's banks have set up RMB clearing mechanism in 21 countries and regions by the end of September, 2016,

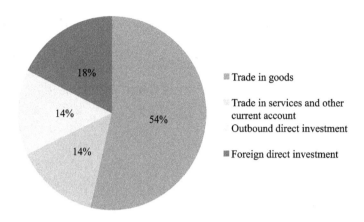

Figure 2   Cross-border RMB settlement in the first 10

months of 2016

Data source: People's Bank of China

covering Southeast Asia, West Europe, Middle East, North
America, South America and Oceania.

Table 1   **Overseas RMB clearing banks**

Country and Region	Time	Overseas RMB clearing banks
Hong Kong, China	December 2003	Bank of China(Hong Kong) Limited
Macao, China	September 2004	Bank of China Macau Branch
Taiwan, China	September 2012	Bank of China Taipei Branch
Singapore	February 2013	ICBC Singapore Branch
UK	June 2014	CCB London Branch
Germany	June 2014	Bank of China Frankfurt Branch
South Korea	July 2014	Bank of Communications Seoul Branch
France	September 2014	Bank of China Paris Branch
Luxembourg	September 2014	ICBC Luxembourg Branch
Qatar	November 2014	ICBC Doha Branch

Country and Region	Time	Overseas RMB clearing banks
Canada	November 2014	ICBC (Canada) Limited
Australia	November 2014	Bank of China Sydney Branch
Malaysia	January 2015	Bank of China (Malaysia) Berhad
Thailand	January 2015	ICBC (Thailand) Limited
Chile	May 2015	CCB Chile Branch
Hungary	June 2015	Bank of China (Hungary) Close Ltd
South Africa	July 2015	Bank of China Johannesburg Branch
Argentina	September 2015	ICBC (Argentina) Limited
Zambia	September 2015	Bank of China(Zambia) Limited
Switzerland	November 2015	CCB Zurich Branch
USA	September 2016	Bank of China New York Branch

Data source: People's Bank of China.

2. Currency Swap and Direct Currency Trading with RMB

The purpose for People's Bank of China to sign currency swap agreements with overseas monetary authorities is not only to maintain regional financial stability but also, more importantly, to facilitate development of bilateral trade and investment. The amount of money for currency swap can be used to support local enterprises' trade and investment so as to promote use of the two sides' currencies in bilateral trade and investment, which will help not only lower the exchange risk that the fluctuation of the dollar will cause in the bilateral international economic activities between both sides of currency swap but also reduce exchange cost to boost bilateral trade and investment.

Since the 2008 global financial crisis, China has kept promoting currency cooperation and signing and renewing bilateral currency swap agreements with overseas central banks or monetary authorities. China has so far signed bilateral currency swap agreements with central banks or monetary authorities from 36 countries and regions including Hong Kong (China), Malaysia, Belarus, Indonesia and South Korea. By the end of 2016, the amount of money that those currency swap agreements actually involved has exceeded 3.1 trillion yuan.

Table 2   Bilateral local currency swap agreements signed between

People's Bank of China and other central banks or monetary authorities

The other party of Swap	Signing time	Swap size	Term
Hong Kong, China	2009. 1. 20	200 bn yuan/ 227 bn HK dollar	3 yrs
	2011. 11. 22 (renewed)	400 bn yuan/490 bn HK dollar (renewed)	
	2014. 11. 22 (renewed)	400 bn yuan / 505 bn HK dollar (renewed)	

The other party of Swap	Signing time	Swap size	Term
Malaysia	2009. 2. 8	80 bn yuan / 40 bn Malaysian ringgit	3 yrs
	2012. 2. 8 (renewed)	180 bn yuan/ 90 bn Malaysian ringgit (renewed)	
	2015. 4. 17 (renewed)	180 bn yuan / 90 bn Malaysian ringgit (renewed)	
Belarus	2009. 3. 11	20 bn yuan / 8 trn Belarusian ruble	3 yrs
	2015. 5. 10 (renewed)	7 bn yuan /16 trn Belarusian ruble (renewed)	
Indonesia	2009. 3. 23	100 bn yuan/ 175 trn Indonesian rupiah	3 yrs
	2013. 10. 1 (renewed)	100 bn yuan/175 trn Indonesian rupiah (renewed)	
Argentina	2009. 4. 2	70 bn yuan/38 bn Argentine peso	3 yrs
	2014. 7. 18 (renewed)	70 bn yuan / 90 bn Argentine peso (renewed)	
South Korea	2009. 4. 20	180 bn yuan / 38 trn South Korean won	3 yrs
	2011. 10. 26 (renewed)	360 bn yuan/64 trn South Korean won (renewed)	
	2014. 10. 11 (renewed)	360 bn yuan / 64 trn South Korean won (renewed)	
Iceland	2010. 6. 9	3. 5 bn yuan/66 bn Icelandic krona	3 yrs
	2013. 9. 11(renewed)	3. 5 bn yuan / 66 bn Icelandic krona (renewed)	
Singapore	2010. 7. 23	150 bn yuan/30 Singapore dollar	3 yrs
	2013. 3. 7(renewed)	300 bn yuan / 60 bn Singapore dollar(renewed)	
	2016. 3. 7(renewed)	300 bn yuan/60 bn Singapore dollar (renewed)	
New Zealand	2011. 4. 18	25 bn yuan/5 bn New Zealand dollar	3 yrs
	2014. 4. 25 (renewed)	25 bn yuan/5 bn New Zealand dollar (renewed)	
Uzbekistan (expired)	2011. 4. 19	0. 7 bn yuan / 167 bn Uzbekistan som	3 yrs

The other party of Swap	Signing time	Swap size	Term
Mongolia	2011. 5. 6	5 bn yuan/1 trn Mongolian tugrik	3 yrs
	2012. 3. 20 (supplemental)	10 bn yuan / 2 trn Mongolian tugrik (expanded)	
	2014. 8. 21 (renewed)	15 bn yuan/4. 5 trn Mongolian tugrik (renewed)	
Kazakhstan	2011. 6. 13	7 bn yuan/150 bn Kazakhstani Tenge	3 yrs
	2014. 12. 14 (renewed)	7 bn yuan/200 bn Kazakhstani Tenge (renewed)	
Thailand	2011. 12. 22	70 bn yuan/320 bn Thailand baht	3 yrs
	2014. 12. 22 (renewed)	70 bn yuan/370 bn Thailand baht (renewed)	
Pakistan	2011. 12. 23	10 bn yuan/140 bn Pakistani rupee	3 yrs
	2014. 12. 23 (renewed)	10 bn yuan/165 bn Pakistani rupee (renewed)	
UAE	2012. 1. 17	35 bn yuan/20 bn UAE dirham	3 yrs
	2015. 12. 14 (renewed)	35 bn yuan/20 bn UAE dirham (renewed)	
Turkey	2012. 2. 21	10 bn yuan/3 bn Turkish lira	3 yrs
	2015. 9. 26 (renewed)	12 bn yuan/5 bn Turkish lira (renewed)	
Australia	2012. 3. 22	200 bn yuan/30 bn Australian dollar	3 yrs
	2015. 3. 30 (renewed)	200 bn yuan/40 bn Australian dollar (renewed)	
Ukraine	2012. 6. 26	15 bn yuan/19 bn Ukrainian hryvna	3 yrs
	2015. 5. 15 (renewed)	15 bn yuan / 54 bn Ukrainian hryvna (renewed)	
Brazil (expired)	2013. 3. 26	190 bn yuan/60 bn Brazilian real	3 yrs
UK	2013. 6. 22	200 bn yuan/20 bn GB pound	3 yrs
	2015. 10. 20 (renewed)	350 bn yuan/35 bn GB pound (renewed)	
Hungary	2013. 9. 9	10 bn yuan/375 bn Hungarian forint	3 yrs
	2016. 9. 12 (renewed)	10 bn yuan/ 416 bn Hungarian forint (renewed)	

（ contd. ）

The other party of Swap	Signing time	Swap size	Term
Albania (expired)	2013. 9. 12	2 bn yuan/35. 8 bn Albanian lek	3 yrs
European Central Bank	2013. 10. 8	350 bn yuan/45 bn European euro	3 yrs
	2016. 9. 27 (renewed)	350 bn yuan/45 bn European euro (renewed)	
Switzerland	2014. 7. 21	150 bn yuan/21 bn Swiss frank	3 yrs
Sri Lanka	2014. 9. 16	10 bn yuan/225 bn Sri Lanka rupee	3 yrs
Russia	2014. 10. 13	150 bn yuan/815 bn Russian rouble	3 yrs
Qatar	2014. 11. 3	35 bn yuan/20. 8 bn Qatar riyal	3 yrs
Canada	2014. 11. 8	200 bn yuan/30 bn Canada dollar	3 yrs
Surinam	2015. 3. 18	1 bn yuan/0. 52 bn Surinamese dollar	3 yrs
Armenia	2015. 3. 25	1 bn yuan/77 bn Armenian dram	3 yrs
South Africa	2015. 4. 10	30 bn yuan/54 bn South African rand	3 yrs
Chile	2015. 5. 25	22 bn yuan/2200 bn Chile peso	3 yrs
Tajikistan	2015. 9. 3	3 bn yuan/3 bn Tajikistani somoni	3 yrs
Morocco	2016. 5. 11	10 bn yuan/15 bn Morocco dihram	3 yrs
Serbia	2016. 6. 17	1. 5 bn yuan/27 bn Serbian dinar	3 yrs
Egypt	2016. 12. 6	18 bn yuan/47 bn Egyptian pound	3 yrs

Data source: People's Bank of China.

In terms of the currency swap agreements that are currently effective, most countries and regions that have signed currency swap agreements with People's Bank of China come from Asia and Pacific area. But in recent years, the number of such countries from Europe, Africa and Latin America also increased gradually. China has signed currency swap agreements with other BRICS countries such as Brazil (expired)、Russia and South Africa, creating favorable conditions for further promotion of use of their own currencies among BRICS countries.

Table 3 **Distribution of countries and regions with which China has signed currency swap agreements**

Areas	Countries or regions
Asia-Pacific Area	Hong Kong(China) , Malaysia, Indonesia, South Korea, Singapore, Uzbekistan(expired) , Mongolia, Kazakhstan, Thailand, Pakistan, UAE, Turkey, Australia, Sri Lanka, Qatar, Tajikistan
Africa	South Africa, Morocco, Egypt
South America	Argentina, Brazil(expired) , Surinam, Chile
Europe	Belarus, Iceland, Ukraine, UK, Hungary, European Central Bank, Switzerland, Russia, Armenia, Serbia, Albania(expired)
North America	Canada
BRICS	Brazil(expired) , Russia, South Africa

Data source: People's Bank of China.

Direct currency trading between RMB and foreign currencies represents another major step forward during the course of RMB internationalization that helps increasing RMB settlement in bilateral trade and investment and raises the international status of RMB. Meanwhile, direct currency trading with RMB can avoid the cost of denominating with the third party currency and reduce the exchange cost of transaction to facilitate bilateral trade, investment and financial cooperation.

Direct currency trading has been developed between RMB and 21 non-US dollar currencies. Since the establishment of the Bretton Woods system, the US dollar has played a central role in the international monetary system as the most important global currency for trade, investment and reserve. Therefore, in the beginning, direct currency trading was developed only between RMB and the US dollar on the back of which indirect currency trade had then been developed between RMB and other currencies. However, the use of US dollar as the medium of exchange both adds to the cost and inconvenience of currency trading between RMB and other foreign currencies and increases the exchange risk for both sides. Therefore, as RMB internationalization presses ahead and foreign economic and trade relations keep growing, it is urgent to establish a direct currency trading mechanism between RMB and other currencies. Hence, since 2010 China Foreign Exchange Trade System has first opened direct currency trading between RMB and Malaysian ringgit and then developed direct currency trading between RMB and 21 non-US dollar currencies including Russian roubble, Japanese yen, Australian dollar, New Zealand dollar, pound, Euro, Singapore dollar, Swiss franc, South African rand, Korean won, UAE dirham, Saudi riyal, Canada dollar.

Table 4   **Direct trading between China and non-US-dollar currencies**

Time	Direct trading currency	Time	Direct trading currency
2010. 8. 19	Ringgit (Malaysia)	2016. 9. 23	Dihram (UAE)
2010. 11. 22	Rouble (Russia)	2016. 9. 23	Riyal (Saudi Arabia)
2012. 5. 29	Yen (Japan)	2016. 11. 11	Canada Dollar (Canada)
2013. 4. 9	Australian Dollar(Australia)	2016. 12. 9	Swedish Krona (Sweden)
2014. 3. 18	New Zealand Dollar (New Zealand)	2016. 12. 9	Norwegian Krone(Norway)
2014. 6. 18	GB Pound (UK)	2016. 12. 9	Turkish Lira (Turkey)
2014. 9. 29	Euro (Euro zone)	2016. 12. 9	Mexican Peso (Mexico)
2014. 10. 27	Singapore Dollar(Singapore)	2016. 12. 9	Hungarian Forint (Hungary)
2015. 11. 9	Swiss Franc (Switzerland)	2016. 12. 9	Danish Krone (Denmark)
2016. 6. 17	Rand (South Africa)	2016. 12. 9	Polish zlty (Poland)
2016. 6. 24	Won (South Korea)		

Data source: China Foreign Exchange Trade System.

3. Construction of Off-shore RMB Financial Centers

Fundamentally speaking, to achieve full RMB internationalization, China must realize financial liberalization and full convertibility of capital account. But the reform of financial liberalization must be carried out step by step. To promote RMB internationalization under the condition of incomplete convertibility of capital account, it is very important to develop offshore RMB financial markets because such offshore markets are needed to provide non-residents holding RMB a platform for RMB-denominated trade, investment and settlement. And offshore markets should be properly separated from onshore markets. By now, RMB offshore financial centers have been set up in Hong Kong, Taibei, Singapore city, London, Frankfurt, Paris, Luxembourg and Toronto to provide RMB investment products in offshore markets through Dim Sum bonds, RQFII, cross-border loans, Shanghai-Hong Kong Stock Connect program and Shenzhen-Hong Kong Stock Connect program. During this process, China expands convertibility of capital account in an orderly and prudential approach.

(1) Dim Sum bonds

Dim Sum bonds refer to offshore bonds issued in Hong Kong by domestic financial institutions and enterprises. China Development Bank issued the first offshore RMB bond in Hong Kong in June 2007, ushering in a new chapter in the development of Dim Sum bond market. After the initial phase of development, Dim Sum bond market witnessed a period of explosive growth between 2010 and 2014. In 2014, issuance of Dim Sum bonds in Hong Kong totalled 183.1 billion yuan, up 89% year-on-year, of which 90% were financial bonds and corporate bonds and more than 75% 1 – 3 year short-term bonds.

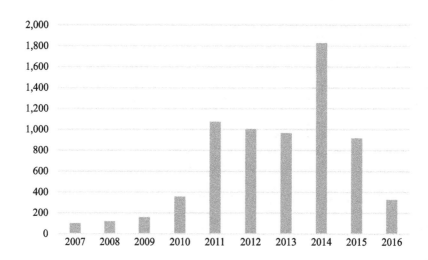

Figure 3   Issuance of Dim Sum bonds (100 million yuan)

Note: Data by December 5, 2016.

Data source: Wind Database.

Table 5   Types and term structure of Hong Kong dim sum bonds

Year	Types				Term				
	Government bonds (100 million yuan)	Financial bonds (100 million yuan)	Corporate bonds (100 million yuan)	Convertible bonds (100 million yuan)	1 yr and shorter (100 million yuan)	1 – 3 yrs (100 million yuan)	3 – 5 yrs (100 million yuan)	5 – 10 yrs (100 million yuan)	10 yrs and longer (100 million yuan)
2007		100.00		58.30		133.30	25.00		

Year	Types				Term				
	Government bonds (100 million yuan)	Financial bonds (100 million yuan)	Corporate bonds (100 million yuan)	Convertible bonds (100 million yuan)	1 yr and shorter (100 million yuan)	1 – 3 yrs (100 million yuan)	3 – 5 yrs (100 million yuan)	5 – 10 yrs (100 million yuan)	10 yrs and longer (100 million yuan)
2008		120.00				120.00			
2009	60.00	100.00		4.47		155.00	9.47		
2010	80.00	176.00	131.60	63.90		341.10	88.40	22.00	
2011	200.00	75.90	948.83	17.72	11.00	869.03	290.22	72.20	
2012	230.00	411.55	363.25	17.73	45.80	731.67	141.56	48.50	55.00
2013	230.00	307.94	428.09	17.95	68.93	597.80	234.05	64.20	19.00
2014	280.00	723.77	827.70	19.30	45.82	1307.30	290.85	192.80	14.00
2015	270.00	400.17	246.94		11.97	497.03	281.86	96.00	30.25
2016	140.00	125.95	62.00	33.50	20.00	254.71	16.74	55.00	15.00

Note: Data by December 5, 2016.

Data source: Wind Database.

After years of stable growth, Dim Sum bonds face new challenges against the pressure of RMB devaluation. Issuance of Dim Sum bonds plummeted between 2015 and 2016. The total Dim Sum issuance volume was 91.7 billion yuan in 2015, roughly half of that in 2014. It declined further in 2016. By December 5, the total Dim Sum issuance volume has reached only 32.7 billion yuan in 2016, basically as much as that in 2010. This fact shows that changing expectation on the foreign exchange rate of RMB is the major driving force behind the fluctuation of the Dim Sum issuance volume.

Dim Sum bonds issued in Hong Kong face three key challenges. The first is the lack of liquidity and a secondary market. Because of its limited market size, Dim Sum bond market is short of market-makers. According to data from the bond quotation website of the Central Moneymarkets Unit (CMU) with the Hong Kong Monetary Authority, all RMB-denominated bonds are not actively traded except the national bonds issued by China's Ministry of Finance, which is traded in the OTC market.

The second challenge is the lack of bond ratings and short maturity, and investors usually prefer to hold short-term bonds. Under the circumstances, offshore RMB-denominated bonds do not have a yield curve of RMB for reference and Hong Kong financial market cannot provide RMB bonds with high liquidity and reasonable duration structure.

The third is that bond issuance is affected by the exchange rate of RMB. As long as the current devaluation expectation exists, investor enthusiasm can hardly return. Inclusion of RMB into SDR and gradually more convertibility under capital account will add to the difficulties of keeping exchange rate stable and thus Dim Sum bond market might shrink further.

(2) RQFII

RQFII refers to RMB Qualified Foreign Institutional Investors. Through RQFII mechanism, overseas institutions can make use of RMB fund raised in offshore markets to invest in China's domestic capital market. On August 17, 2011, the then Vice Premier Li Keqiang said at a forum in Kong Kong that RMB Qualified Foreign Institutional Investors will be allowed to invest in the domestic securities market with a starting quota of 20 billion yuan.

Since then, qualified foreign institutional investors have gradually accelerated their participation in the domestic securities market under RQFII mechanism. In recent years, as RMB internationalization moves ahead and restrictions on asset allocation are gradually removed, investment through RQFII have increased steadily. RQFII invested 4599. 2 billion yuan in 2015, on average 383. 2 billion yuan per month, while having opened 942 accounts in China's A-share market by the end of 2015. In 2016, RQFII basically continued the momentum of steady growth of the previous year, investing 4,947. 9 billion yuan in the first ten months and having opened 1,067 accounts in the A-share market by the end of October.

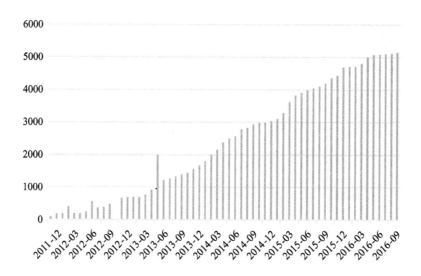

Figure 4　RQFII investment（100 million yuan）

Data source: Wind Database.

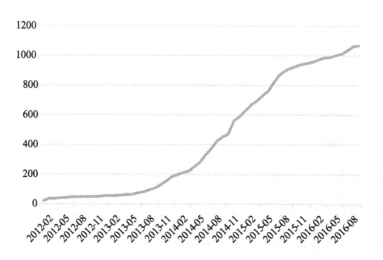

Figure 5　RQFII's A-share accounts

Data source: Wind Database.

During the two-day China-US Strategic and Economic Dialogue in June 2016, Yi Gang, deputy governor of People's Bank of China, indicated that China would provide the US with RQFII quota of 250 billion yuan (US $ 38 billion). This is the first time that China has provided the US with such a quota, a milestone for RMB internationalization and RQFII mechanism.

Research shows that most quota of RQFII are used by institutional investors from Hong Kong. There are mainly two explanations. One is that Hong Kong funds tend to allocate most of their assets in Asia Pacific areas and have high demand for domestic RQFII while funds from UK, France and Germany prefer to global asset allocation and have relatively few demand for the domestic stock market. The other is that investors from other regions can hardly understand complex regulatory measures over RQFII. According to the approval process of RQFII, China Securities Regulatory Commission is responsible for approving the qualification of RQFII and the State Administration of Foreign Exchange will approve the total quota for a certain region and specific quota for each financial institution. For overseas investors, each RQFII business will face restrictions over institutional qualification, approval of quota and structure of products. Since

Hong Kong banks and investors have done more businesses related to the domestic market, they are able to interpret such regulations in a more flexible way. If the RQFII mechanism is to be further expanded, it is necessary to further streamline its regulatory and approval system.

(3) Cross-border RMB Loans

Cross-border RMB loans is one of the measures that the Chinese government has taken to enable overseas financial institutions to channel overseas RMB back into the domestic market, ensuring use of RMB as a settlement currency to meet real trade and investment demand. In January 2013, Qianhai has become the first region in China to provide cross-border RMB loans, marking a new milestone in RMB internationalization. With construction of Qianhai being accelerated, the scope and procedure of RMB settlement in cross-border trade has been gradually expanded and optimized and the size of cross-border RMB loans has grown rapidly in Qianhai. By the end of March 2015, the registered volume of cross-border RMB loans in Qianhai had reached 91. 1 billion yuan with 22. 8 billion yuan having been withdrawn. The two figures in 2013 were 14. 8 billion yuan and 3. 36 billion yuan respectively. By now, more than 30 central SOEs and industrial leaders including China Everbright International, China Guangdong Nuclear Power Group, China Resources (Holdings), China Shipbuilding Industry Corporation, the S. F Express Company, Industrial Bank Financial Leasing Company, China Poly Group, China Gezhouba Group, HSAE, Guangxi Nonferrous Metals Group, Shenzhen MTC, Shenzhen Tianyuan Dic Information Technology Company, Longgang City Investment, Baoan Construction Investment Group, and China Aerospace Science and Industry Corp have entered Qianhai to engage in cross-border loan business for the support of low-cost capital. Based on the pilot program of cross-border RMB loans in Qianhai, the Chinese government has since extended such pilot programs to Xiamen, Quanzhou Experimental Area of Comprehensive Financial Reform and Fujian (Pilot) Free Trade Zone.

In December 2014, Qianhai Financial Holdings and 6 financial institutions from Shenzhen and Hong Kong arranged the first cross-border RMB syndicated loan in Qianhai, marking the debut and pricing of "Qianhai Concept" and cross-border RMB syndicated loan in Hong Kong interbank market, another milestone in cross-border RMB loans. Now, enterprises in Qianhai can not only raise funds from Hong Kong banks through overseas loans under domestic guarantee and direct loans but also obtain cross-border financing through syndicated loans. The arrangement of cross-border financing can significantly cut loan interest rates for enterprises. RMB loans that enterprises obtained from overseas financial institutions are priced according to market interest rates in Hong Kong the level of which is about 10% below the benchmark interest rates set by the central bank in the domestic market. And such loans have opened a channel of overseas financing for enterprises, especially large enterprises.

In comparison with the registered volume, the actual amount of loans that have been withdrawn are yet to be increased. In fact, as overseas RMB interest rates climb, the cost of cross-border RMB financing has also risen to shrink the price advantage of cross-border RMB loans.

In addition, the target clients of cross-border loans in Qianhai are enterprises registered in Qianhai most of which are newly set up and have only limited size and credit. Hong Kong banks usually can provide loans to them only with guarantee from domestic banks. Hence, it is more than often that only enterprises with high qualifications can obtain loans while small and medium-sized enterprises have little access to low-cost loans. In principle, it takes only two work weeks to get loans registered and granted. But the actual procedure for enterprises to withdraw loans is much more time-consuming. That Hong Kong banks have strict requirements over the usage, cost and term of loans also, to a certain extent, adds to the cost of guarantee and thus the cost of loans for enterprises. Besides the price factor, business insiders pointed out that another reason why the amount of funds withdrawn from cross-border loans in Qianhai is limited is the single source of capital provided only by banks in Hong Kong.

(4) Shanghai-Hong Kong Stock Connect

Shanghai-Hong Kong Stock Connect program refers to the scheme that Shanghai Stock Exchange and the Stock Exchange of Hong Kong permit investors from both sides to trade designated shares on the other market using their local clearing houses (or brokers). It is an investment channel that connects stock markets in Shanghai and Hong Kong. On April 10, 2014, China Securities Regulatory Commission (CSRC) officially approved the pilot stock connect program. The CSRC noted that the total quota for Shanghai-Hong Kong Stock Connect program is 550 billion yuan and the capital account balance of each individual investor participating the program should be no less than 500,000 yuan.

Shanghai-Hong Kong Stock Connect program includes two parts: the part of Shanghai stock connect refers to that investors can trade designated shares listed on Shanghai Stock Exchange by using Hong Kong dealers and the stock trading service company set up by the Stock Exchange of Hong Kong; the part of Hong Kong stock connect refers to that investors can trade designated shares listed on the Stock Exchange of Hong Kong by using domestic securities firms and the stock trading service company set up by Shanghai Stock Exchange.

As a major innovation of the two-way opening-up of China's capital market, "Shanghai-Hong Kong Stock Connect" has achieved maximum market effect with minimum institutional cost. The design of the principle of locality and close-ended settlement in the program has allowed investors from both sides to invest in the other market while using, to the maximum extent, laws, rules and trade habits in their own market. This marks the first step of two-way opening-up of China's capital market under the condition of regulatory transparency and rick control.

By November 2016, Shanghai-Hong Kong Stock Connect has had an aggregate trade volume of 3,565.751 billion yuan among which Hong Kong stock connect contributed 1,23.909 billion yuan and Shanghai stock connect 2301.843 billion yuan. A review of the achievement of "Shanghai-Hong Kong Stock Connect" shows that, though the overall trade volume is not as large as expected, the program has operated smoothly, standing the test of the volatile fluctuation in the A-share market while providing a replicable sample for other programs such as Shenzhen-Hong Kong Stock Connect and Shanghai-London Stock Connect.

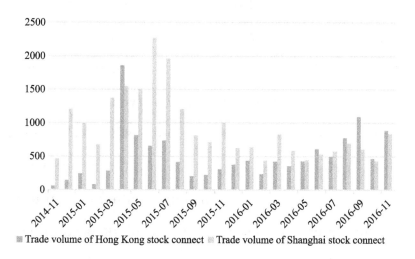

Figure 6   Trade volume of Shanghai-Hong Kong Stock Connect

(100 **million yuan**)

Data source: Wind Database.

(5) Shenzhen-Hong Kong Stock Connect

Shenzhen-Hong Kong Stock Connect refers to the technology connect built between Shenzhen Stock Exchange and the Stock Exchange of Hong Kong that enable domestic and Hong Kong investors to trade designated shares on the other market by using local securities firms or dealers. On December 5, 2016, Shenzhen-Hong Kong Stock Connect was officially launched. As Li Xiaojia, CEO of Hong Kong Stock Exchanges and Clearing, pointed out at the opening ceremony, if Shanghai-Hong Kong Stock Connect is the first step of inter-connectivity, now Shenzhen-Hong Kong Stock Connect marks the second step. Shenzhen-Hong Kong Stock Connect has replicated the successful experience of the pilot Shanghai-Hong Kong Stock Connect and served as another connectivity mechanism between the domestic stock exchange and that in Hong Kong. The launch of Shenzhen-Hong Kong Stock Connect is another major and meaningful step forward in boosting inter-connectivity between the domestic financial market and that of Hong Kong.

According to official statement, Shenzhen Stock Exchange announced on November 25 altogether 417 shares under Shenzhen-Hong Kong Stock Connect program including 100 from Hong Seng Composite Largecap Index, 193 from Hong Seng Composite Midcap Index, 95 from Hong Seng Composite Smallcap Index and 29 A + H shares beyond these indexes. These shares accounted for 87% of the total market valuation of the Stock Exchange of Hong Kong and 91% of the average daily trade volume. On the same day, the Stock Exchange of Hong Kong announced 881 shares under Shenzhen-Hong Kong Stock Connect program including 267 from the Main Board of Shenzhen Stock Exchange, 411 from the Small and Medium Enterprise Board and 203 from the Growth Enterprise Board, altogether accounting for 71% of the total market valuation of Shenzhen's A-Share market and 66% of the average daily trade volume.

Till the end of October 2016, more than 1,860 companies have been listed in Shenzhen Stock Exchange with a total market valuation of about 23 trillion yuan. By now, the trade volume has reached 64 trillion yuan, ranking high among all stock exchanges around the world. And the collective characteristic of listed companies in Shenzhen Stock Exchange is innovation and growth.

In retrospect, on the opening day of Shanghai-Hong Kong Stock Connect, investors' great interest to buy shares at Shanghai stock market contrasts sharply with their lack of interest about buying shares at Hong Kong Stock market. The former indicated that the attraction of the A-share market was far bigger than the Hong Hong stock market at that time and a leveraged bull had just started. Two years later, against the background of mounting deprecation pressure on RMB, it is hard to tell where the A-share market will go and if the old success can be repeated.

4. Opening-up of Interbank Market and Issuance of Panda Bond

(1) Opening-up of China's interbank market

In a sense, the process of RMB internationalization is the process to open China's capital account. By analyzing the opening-up of interbank market, we can clearly see cooperation between RMB internationalization and opening-up of capital account.

China's interbank market is composed of bond market (including securitization products), paper market, foreign exchange market and interbank loan market. For RMB internationalization, bond market is the most important one. Hence, the interbank market discussed below is mainly about bond market. During the course of RMB internationalization, a key problem has arisen as more and more RMB flew into overseas markets and were held by non-residents that is how to provide non-residents with ample RMB investment channels. International experience indicates that the most important investment channel for an international currency is the capital market of the issuing country including the bond market and the stock market. In terms of promoting RMB internationalization, opening-up of China's interbank market is to provide non-residents with investment channel to RMB-denominated bonds.

For currency internationalization, the more important value of opening-up of interbank market is to promote the currency to become an international reserve currency. One of the key symbols of successful currency internationalization is that the currency has become an international reserve currency as the US dollar, euro and pound did. Most international reserve currencies will not be saved in the form of cash but exist in the form of bonds denominated with these currencies. And these bonds have three characteristics: First, they have high credit rating and low default risk; Second, they have better return on investment than cash; Third, they boasts high liquidity and can be easily converted into cash. Bonds with these three characteristics will become global safe assets and thus investment targets for many countries as international reserves. From a long-term perspective, opening-up of China's interbank market is also the process to promote RMB-denominated bonds to become global safe assets and thus make RMB an international reserve currency.

I. History of the opening-up of the interbank bond market

China began to open the domestic bond market to overseas institutions in August 2010 when People's Bank of China adopted a pilot policy to allow foreign central banks or monetary authorities, overseas clearing banks for RMB business, and overseas participating banks for RMB settlement of cross-border trade to invest in the interbank bond market with RMB funds. The scope of investors has since been gradually expanded.

Between 2011 and 2012, China Securities Regulatory Commission and People's Bank of China have released new rules to allow QFII/RQFII to enter the interbank market but the approval procedure remains time-consuming. In March, 2013, after issuing "Notice on issues concerning investment in the interbank bond market by qualified foreign institutional investors", People's Bank of China began to accelerate approval of the entry of QFII/RQFII into the interbank market.

In June 2015, People's Bank of China allowed overseas clearing banks for RMB business and overseas participating banks for RMB settlement of cross-border trade to invest in repo. In July 2015, People's Bank of China loosened rules on investment in the interbank bond market by three types of sovereign institutions including foreign central banks or monetary authorities, international financial organization and sovereign wealth funds by abolishing ex-ante approval of access and quota and expanding the scope of investment to include cash bond, bond repurchase, securities lending, bond forward, interest rate swap and forward rate agreement.

Since the beginning of 2016, People's Bank of China has considerably accelerated opening-up of the interbank bond market in terms of expanding the scope of investors and investment products. In February 2016, China extended access to the interbank bond market to more foreign institutional investors including overseas commercial banks, insurance companies, securities firms, fund management companies and other asset management agencies. It also clarified the entry procedure and regulatory measures for foreign central banks and similar institutions, restating that overseas institutional investors are subject to registration management; quota approval is abolished; foreign central banks and similar institutions do not need authorization or approval

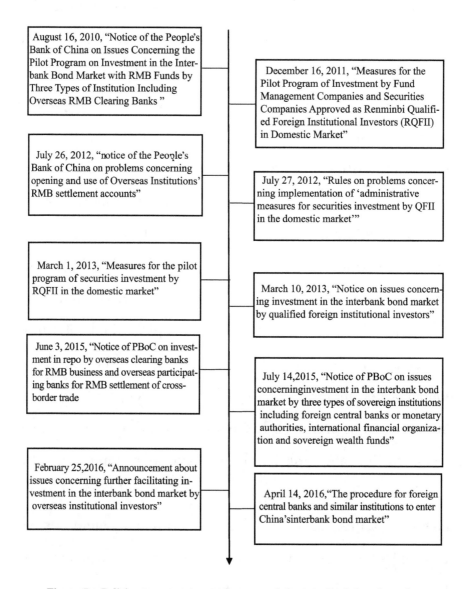

Figure 7   Policies to promote opening – up of the interbank bond market

Data source: websites of People's Bank of China and China Securities Regulatory Commission for outward remittances of funds related to their securities and foreign exchange investment. In April, China's central bank issued the procedure for foreign central banks and similar institutions to enter the interbank bond market and foreign exchange market, including more opening-up in terms of investment quota, investment products and free remittance of funds. By October 2016, 207 foreign commercial banks, non-bank financial institutions, investment managers of financial institutions and other institutional investors have entered China's interbank bond market.

II. Transactions of foreign institutional investors in the interbank market

As China accelerated the pace of RMB internationalization and opened up its interbank market, the number of foreign investors in China's interbank market has increased rapidly since 2010. By analyzing statistics from People's Bank of China, this report finds that the open interest held by foreign institutions and their trade volume are growing amid fluctuation. In terms of the type of bonds, foreign institutional investors mainly hold rate securities among which government bonds and policy bank bonds accounted for more than 90%. In terms of trade volume, foreign investors have taken an increasingly big share of the interbank market with their open interest reaching 747. 128 billion yuan, about 2.5% of the total depository trust in the market. In terms of spot trading of bonds, the transaction volume has increased

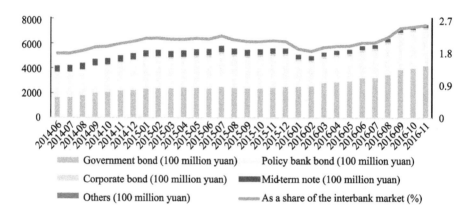

Figure 8   Bonds held by overseas institutions and their market share

Data source: People's Bank of China.

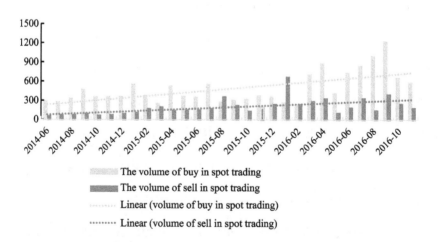

Figure 9   The volume of spot trading of bonds by overseas institutions in the interbank market (100 million yuan)

Data source: People's Bank of China.

year by year while the volume of buy is rising amid fluctuation and the volume of sell remains flat. The following figure clearly shows that there is an obvious rise in the total trading volume by foreign institutions in the interbank bond market.

According to statistics from People's Bank of China, by the end of November 2016, 56% of all the bonds held by foreign institutions are government bonds, 39% are policy bank bonds (among which bonds issued by China Development Bank, Agricultural Development Bank of China and Export-Import Bank of China accounted for 21% , 10% and 8% respectively), 3% and 2% are medium-term notes and corporate bonds, and the total of government bonds they held has reached 168. 3 billion yuan. A research report by China International Capital Corporation Limited shows that the low proportion of credit bonds held by foreign institutions is related to their strict risk control over cross-border investment. Since the credibility of domestic credit rating agencies is not well accepted in the international market, most foreign institutions only invest in sovereign rating products. As the composition of foreign institutional investors became more diversified in recent years, the amount of corporate bonds and medium-term notes they held went up too. The amount of corporate bonds they held increased from

6. 987 billion yuan at the end of 2013 to 15. 899 billion yuan by the end of November 2016 while that of medium-term notes soared from zero to 18. 862 billion yuan.

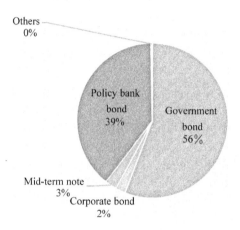

Figure 10   The composition of bonds held by foreign investors in the

interbank market (by November 2016)

Data source : People's Bank of China.

(2) Issuance of Panda Bond

Panda Bond refers to RMB-denominated foreign bonds that foreign institutions issued in China. China began the pilot program of panda bonds in October 2005 when International Finance Corporation and Asian Development Bank had issued RMB-denominated bonds worth of 1. 13 billion yuan and 1 billion yuan respectively to set a precedent for foreign institutions to issue panda bonds in this country. However, because of regulatory restrictions over issuance approval and usage of fund, the panda bond market developed slowly in following years. Between 2005 and 2014, the total issuance of the panda bond market was only 6 billion yuan.

As RMB internationalization accelerated, regulatory policies have been changed to boost development of the panda bond market. The scope of issuers has been expanded; cross-border use of funds raised from bond issuance and funds for paying interest and principal are allowed for foreign institutions and rules on cross-border RMB settlement has been made clear; a domestic-international dual rating system has been adopted; use of accounting and auditing methods which are in accordance with domestic accounting standards and approved by China's Ministry of Finance has been allowed. In March 2014, Germany's Daimler AG successfully issued one-year Private Publication Notes in the interbank market to become the first foreign non-financial corporate that has issued debt financing instruments in China's interbank market. In 2015, the National Development and Reform Commission, the Ministry of Foreign Affairs and the Ministry of Commerce jointly issued " Vision and Actions on Jointly Building Silk Road Economic Belt and 21st-Century Maritime Silk Road", stressing that "We will support the efforts of governments of the countries along the Belt and Road and their companies and financial institutions with good credit-rating to issue Renminbi bonds in China. " In September 2015, HSBC and Bank of China (Hong Kong) successfully issued the first panda bond issued by foreign financial institutions in the domestic interbank bond market. In December 2015, the government of South Korea issued the first sovereign panda bond worth 3 billion yuan to become the first foreign government allowed to issue RMB-denominated bonds in China. Driven by both policy support and declining interest rates, the panda bond market has expanded rapidly as both the scope of issuers and the size of bond issuance have been enlarged. The issu-

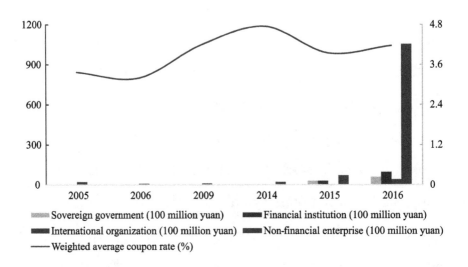

Figure 11 **Statistics on the size of issuance of Panda bonds between**

2005 **and November** 2016

Data source: Wind Database.

ance of panda bonds totaled 13 billion yuan in 2015 and has soared to 124. 82 billion yuan in the first 11 months of 2016.

By the end of November in 2016, altogether 36 foreign enterprises, international organizations and sovereign governments have issued 79 panda bonds through public or private publication in the interbank bond market and the exchange bond market, including commercial paper, medium-term note, private publication note, commercial bank bond, international institutional bond, corporate bond and private bond. Panda bonds have gradually developed into a new channel of diversified financing for foreign institutions.

Table 6   **Types of Panda Bonds**

Location of listing	Bond types	Number of issuance	Percentage	Size of issuance (100 million yuan)	Percentage
Interbank bond market	Commercial paper	5	6. 33	51. 00	3. 55
	Mid-term note	7	8. 86	180. 00	12. 52
	Private publication note	9	11. 39	180. 00	12. 52
	Commercial bank bond	5	6. 33	46. 00	3. 20
	International institutional bond	9	11. 39	170. 00	11. 82

Location of listing		Bond types	Number of issuance	Percentage	Size of issuance (100 million yuan)	Percentage
Exchange bond market	Shanghai	Corporate bond	14	17. 72	182. 00	12. 65
		Private bond	27	34. 18	586. 40	40. 77
	Shenzhen	Private bond	3	3. 80	42. 80	2. 98
Total			79	100. 00	1438. 20	100. 00

Data source: Wind Database.

Ⅰ. Characteristics of the issuers and debt ratings in the Panda Bond market

Debt rating is an important condition for bond issuance. Because China's Panda Bond market is still in its early development, some fund-raisers that it has attracted have not got debt rating in the initial phase of issuance. Among all the panda bonds with debt rating, 83% are granted AAA by domestic or international rating agencies while 15% and 1.6% are granted AA + and AA respectively. In terms of the size of issuance and coupon rate, like other types of bonds, the higher the debt rating is, the more proceeds the issuance will raise and the lower the coupon rate will be.

Table 7   **Debt rating and issuance of Panda bond**

Debt rating	2005 – 2014			2015			The first 11 months of 2016		
	Number of issuance	Size of issuance (100 millon yuan)	Weighed coupon rate (%)	Number of issuance	Size of issuance (100 millon yuan)	Weighed coupon rate (%)	Number of issuance	Size of issuance (100 millon yuan)	Weighed coupon rate (%)
AAA	2	20	3. 77	6	75	3. 45	41	837	4. 12
AA +				2	5	7. 10	7	141	5. 19
AA							1	6. 8	7. 50
None	4	40	4. 03	3	50	4. 35	13	263. 40	3. 58

Data source: Wind Database.

Ⅱ. Term structure and average coupon rate of Panda Bond

The term structure of bonds is a key element to gauge the development of the bond market. Among all the 79 panda bonds issued, the term of most early-issued panda bonds is shorter than 5 years. But long-term debts with a term of 6 to 10 years are increasing in the past year. According to Shanghai Brilliance Credit Rating & Investor Service Company, this is related to not only the fact that issuers are testing with short-term bonds and high-frequency issuance but also the industrial cycle of the issuers. [1]In terms of the cou-

---

[1] Manxi Cao(2016): "Panda Bond Development in the Perspective of International Market", Shanghai Brilliance credit Rating & Investors Service Co. Ltd..

pon rate of panda bonds, the weighted coupon rate of long-term bonds was higher than that of short-term bonds before 2015. Since 2016, a positive correlation between the weighted coupon rate and the term of bonds has come into being, given the long-term trend of interest rates.

Table 8   **Term structure and issuance of Panda bond**

Year	2 yrs and shorter			3 – 5 yrs			6 – 10 yrs		
	Number of issuance	Size of issuance (hundred millon yuan)	Weighed coupon rate (%)	Number of issuance	Size of issuance (hundred millon yuan)	Weighed coupon rate (%)	Number of issuance	Size of issuance (hundred millon yuan)	Weighed coupon rate (%)
2005 – 2014	2	20.00	4.75				4	40.00	3.54
2015	4	55.00	4.23	7	75.00	3.74			
2016	8	217.00	3.23	11	796.90	4.23	40	48.18	4.83

Data source: Wind Database.

III. Industrial structure of Panda Bond

In terms of the industrial distribution of the issuers of panda bonds, the issuers have covered 9 major industries including real estate sector, construction, transportation, warehouse and postal service, finance and manufacturing. Among them, real estate sector, manufacturing and finance rank among the largest issuers while the number of their issuance accounted for 34% , 20% and 19% of the total and the size of their issuance 42% , 21% and 14% of the total respectively.

Unlike other foreign bond markets, China's Panda Bond market has far more and larger bond issuance from real estate and construction sectors than from the financial sector. This is determined by the micro structure of market players under China's economic environment that many foreign-funded companies lack diversified channels for financing. Take the Wharf (Holdings) as an example. This company has expanded its business into the domestic market for more than a decade, with its domestic assets exceeding 100 billion yuan. Due to restrictions of previous loan policies, its RMB-denominated debts amounted to only 4 to 5 billion yuan. Such a low proportion of RMB debts and limited channel to raise funds from the domestic market have seriously hindered the development of this company. [1]Since RMB internationalization accelerated in 2015, China's regulators have gradually opened up the domestic bond market, providing a new and standardized channel of financing for foreign-funded companies.

---

[1] "Foreign Capital Real Estate Enterprises Issue Panda Bonds, Accelenating RMB Internationalization", *China Business News Day*, A05 , Oct. 20, 2016.

It is also noteworthy that, though the panda bond market belongs to international bond markets in which foreign institutions constitute the majority of the financing party, most issuers from real estate and manufacturing sectors actually come from the Chinese mainland and Hong Kong, such as China Merchants Group (Hong Kong) Limited and HNA Group (International) Limited which are registered in Hong Kong and China Resources Land Limited, Country Garden, and Shimao Property Holding Limited which are registered in Cayman Islands. More efforts are needed to explore how to attract more countries and foreign institutions to issue bonds

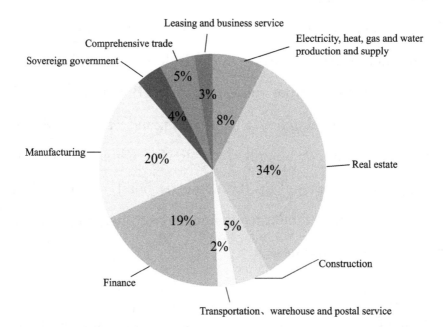

Figure 12 The industrial distribution (issuance) of Panda bonds
Data source: Wind Database.

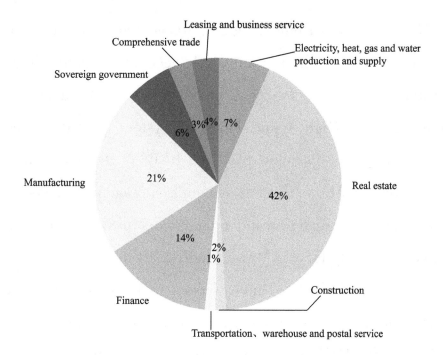

Figure 13   **The issuing scale of Panda bonds**

Data source: Wind Database.

in the panda bond market, diversify the structure of issuers and promote use of RMB settlement in cross-border trade.

5. Construction of RMB Settlement System for Cross-border Transaction

A settlement system for cross-border payment is infrastructure construction for internationalization of a currency. China's original RMB settlement for cross-border payment relied mainly on the two channels of clearing banks for

RMB business in Hong Kong and Macao and domestic agency banks both of which would settle accounts by using China National Advanced Payment System (CNAPS), a system consisting of High Value Payment System (HVPS) and Bulk Electronic Payment System (BEPS). Overseas banks will open RMB settlement accounts in agency banks or clearing banks and transmit cross-border payment information via Society for Worldwide Interbank Financial Telecommunication (SWIFT). Due to factors such as the time lapse for running the system and translation of code, the original channel for RMB cross-border settlement is not very efficient. Besides, CNAPS cannot separate domestic interbank payment from cross-border RMB payment settlement to ensure the safety of the system.

Since it launched pilot cross-border RMB business in 2009, China has already done cross-border RMB payment business with 174 countries. The amount of RMB settlement in cross-border trade has soared from less than 200 billion yuan in 2010 to 4.4 trillion yuan in the first ten months of 2016, making it impossible to fully meet the need for development of RMB business with CNAPS. It is necessary to integrate the existing RMB payment clearing channel and resources and enhance infrastructure construction for the financial system. To ensure safety, stability and efficiency of RMB cross-border payment settlement, People's Bank of China has begun to establish Cross-Border Interbank Payment System (CIPS) in 2012 in line with "Principles for Financial Infrastructure". The CIPS (Phase I) was officially put into operation on October 8, 2015[1].

The main functions of CIPS (Phase I) include providing settlement for RMB cross-border payment by domestic and foreign institutions and supporting RMB cross-border settlement, cross-border direct investment, cross-border financing and personal remittance in the financial market. CIPS can provide participants with highly efficient cross-border, cross-time-zone, cross-currency payment settlement via its connection with HVPS.

CIPS (Phase I) has raised efficiency of settlement in following aspects: first, CIPS (Phase I) processes client remittances and remittances by financial institutions in real-time gross settlement with liquidity support from HVPS and interbank lending. Second, CIPS provide domestic direct

---

[1] Construction of CIPS is carried out in two phases, and CIPS (Phase I) provides real-time gross settlement for cross-border trade settlement, cross-border direct investment and other cross-border RMB settlement. CIPS (Phase II) will provide mixed settlement that is more liquidity-saving to comprehensively support RMB cross-border and offshore settlement.

participants with special line access that allows them to have one-point access, concentrate settlement and shorten path of settlement. Third, by adopting the internationally-recognized ISO20022 standard for financial services messaging and using the unified and standardized Chinese Commercial Code, CIPS has taken into full consideration the need of code switching with the current SWIFT code to support transmission in both Chinese and English so as to raise the speed of code-switching. Fourth, the operation period of CIPS has been extended from 9:00 to 20:00 to meet the need of the development of RMB business in multiple time zones.

6. Summary

Between 2009 and 2016, RMB internationalization made remarkable progress because of the urgent demand from the international community for a diversified international monetary system, China's policy support and appreciation expectation on RMB. In October 2016, RMB was officially included into the SDR currency bracket by the International Monetary Fund, highlighting global recognition of the achievements of RMB internationalization over the past years.

In summary, the achievements of RMB internationalization include following aspects.

First, RMB cross-border settlement under current account has developed rapidly. The absolute size of RMB settlement in cross-border trade has soared from 3.6 billion yuan in the fourth quarter of 2009 to 1.3 trillion yuan in the third quarter of 2016. Due to impact of the European debt crisis, the growth of RMB settlement in cross-border trade had stopped between the second half of 2011 and early 2012 but rebounded rapidly between 2012 and 2013. In March, 2014, after the daily range of RMB exchange rate fluctuation was enlarged from 1% to 2%, the size of RMB settlement in cross-border trade began to fluctuate vehemently. Since the "August 11" foreign exchange reform in 2015, the growth of RMB settlement in cross-border trade has decelerated significantly. As a key base of intermediary trade for domestic enterprises to take part in the global trade, Hong Kong has played a major role in RMB settlement in cross-border trade. Between the fourth quarter of 2009 and the first quarter of 2015, about 80% of RMB settlements in cross-border trade are done through Hong Kong.

Second, RMB cross-border business under capital account has been making breakthroughs. There are more and more channels for inward RMB cross-border flow including RQFII (RMB Qualified Foreign Institutional Investor), RF-DI (RMB foreign direct investment), the entry of three types of foreign institutions into the interbank bond market, RMB cross-border loans and Shanghai-Hong Kong Stock Connect. Channels for outward RMB cross-border flow under capital account mainly include RQDII (RMB Qualified Domestic Institutional Investor), RODI (RMB Overseas Direct Investment) and enterprises' RMB loans to overseas subsidiary companies among which RFDI and RQFII are the main channels for inward flow of overseas RMB under capital account. In the third quarter of 2016, China's RMB settlement in cross-border direct investment amounted to 1. 8 trillion yuan among which RODI and RFDI accounted for 830 billion yuan and 1. 004 trillion yuan respectively. By Nov. 2016, the Chinese mainland has approved an aggregate RQFII quota of 329. 8 billion yuan for 6 countries and regions. China Securities Regulatory Commission will further deepen reform of the RQFII mechanism to break the quota limit of 1 billion dollar and facilitate inward and outward flow of capital.

Third, construction of off shore RMB markets is proceeding a pace. Offshore RMB markets develop rapidly. Hong Kong has become the most important RMB off shore center in the world and RMB business is booming in Singapore city, Taipei, London, Luxembourg, Paris and Frankfurt. RMB clearing banks can be found in major financial trading market in Asia, Europe, America, Africa and Oceania. In October 2015, People Bank of China set up CIPS, a key infrastructure for RMB internationalization, to facilitate RMB cross-border and offshore business for domestic and foreign financial institutions. The amount of RMB deposits in Hong Kong had increased from less than 100 billion yuan in July 2010 to 662. 5 billion yuan in October 2016. This is a result of the role that Hong Kong plays as the most important intermediary trade port for the mainland as well as cooperation between People's Bank of China and Hong Kong Monetary Authority to substantially expand the scope for RMB business in Hong Kong by adopting a series of supportive policies. However, like RMB settlement in cross-border trade, the growth of RMB deposits in Hong Kong had once turned negative between the second half of 2011 and early 2012. After the "August 11" foreign exchange reform in 2015, RMB deposits in Hong Kong witnessed massive negative growth. It is noteworthy that among

RMB deposits in Hong Kong, the proportion of term deposits climbed from 30% in 2009 to about 83% in 2016, indicating that RMB deposits in Hong Kong originate from the outflow of fund from cross-border trade settlement and have inadequate financial investment instruments.

RMB internationalization has achieved remarkable progress but its foundation for development is not solid. According to statistics from SWIFT, RMB has become the fifth largest global payment currency, ranking only behind dollar, euro, pound and yen and boasting a market share of 4%. According to a survey by Bank for International Settlement, the proportion of RMB in global transaction volume has increased from 0.1% in 2004 to 4% in 2016 while its ranking rose from the 35th to the 8th. Clearly, RMB has assumed a crucial role in the international monetary system. But one of the key driving forces to promote RMB internationalization under the condition of incomplete convertibility of capital account is the spread of foreign exchange rates and interest rates between domestic and overseas markets. As the exchange rate of RMB approaches the equilibrium level, the spread of foreign exchange rates between domestic and overseas markets gradually disappeared. And the expansion of the daily range of RMB exchange rate fluctuation has further diminished the room for exchange rate arbitrage between domestic and overseas markets. Before RMB internationalization becomes an inherent driving force, it is unavoidable that the process will suffer short-term turbulence and even setbacks.

After the "August 11" foreign exchange reform, RMB internationalization had been in the doldrums for a while. The average growth rate of RMB settlement in cross-border trade was 55% between 2010 and 2014 while that of RMB deposits in Hong Kong reached 120%. Nevertheless, between the "August 11" foreign exchange reform and October 2016, the monthly total of RMB cross-border settlement declined from 775 billion yuan to 360 billion yuan, on average down 30% per month over the same period last year. Meanwhile, the amount of RMB deposits in Hong Kong dropped from 1 trillion yuan to 662. 5 billion yuan, on average down 25% per month over the same period last year. The new issuance of dim sum bonds in 2016 was 46. 9 billion yuan and its growth rate declined by 50%. There are mainly three reasons why RMB internationalization was in the doldrums.

First, expansion of the daily range of RMB exchange rate fluctuation and the change of expectation over RMB appreciation had diminished the space for cross-border exchange rate arbitrage. Between September 2012 and March 2014, RMB central parity was fixed relatively lower than onshore and offshore spot rates and onshore spot rate was also relatively lower than offshore spot rate, indicating strong expectation over RMB appreciation. In March 2014, the daily range of RMB exchange rate fluctuation was enlarged to 2% in both directions. Since then, RMB appreciation expectation has plummeted. After the "August 11" foreign exchange reform, onshore spot rate began to be higher than offshore exchange rate and RMB depreciation expectation emerged. Within just a year, RMB appreciation expectation was replaced by strong devaluation expectation, and a large part of RMB internationalization business based on cross-border arbitrage also declined.

Though the proportion of RMB settlement in cross-border trade has kept rising, RMB settlement does not necessarily mean that the trade is RMB-denominated. When the exchange rate of RMB turned from appreciation to depreciation, many domestic importers who had used RMB for settlement would be required by their foreign counterparts to pay in US dollar while domestic exporters were required by foreign counterparts to allow payment in RMB. Besides, when offshore RMB is cheaper, many domestic exporters incline to use US dollar for settlement in offshore markets and then recycle RMB back into the domestic market. Historical data showed that the accumulation of offshore RMB deposits in Hong Kong was largely a result of RMB cross-border arbitrage. As RMB appreciation expectation is gone and two-way fluctuation of RMB exchange rate widens, there will be less such arbitrage and hence less offshore RMB deposits in Hong Kong.

Second, the cyclical rise of US dollar will reduce the attractiveness of RMB while both domestic and overseas players will like to hold more US dollars. In 2015, the third quarter statistics showed that the proportion of banks buying foreign exchange to their total foreign receipts declined to 43% while their selling foreign exchange accounted for 67% of their total foreign payment. This indicated that enterprises were more willing to hold US dollars. On the one hand, because the US dollar is on the track of appreciation and overseas exporters prefer settlement in US dollar, Chinese enterprises and importers need to buy foreign exchange from banks for payment and the proportion of bank selling foreign exchange to their foreign payment has thus significantly increased. On the other hand, because of the relative depreciation of offshore RMB in Hong Kong against onshore RMB, it pays for enterprises to buy foreign exchange in the Chinese mainland. As a result, the purchase of foreign exchange by enterprises has increased while their sale of foreign exchange to banks declined.

Third, as the RMB financing cost gap between overseas and domestic markets narrows, dim sum bonds become less attractive to domestic enterprises. In the international monetary system, RMB is still a risk currency. In their currency arbitrage strategies, investors tend to use Japanese yen or US dollar as the financing currency and choose Australian dollar or emerging market currencies as the investment currency. As a high-yield risk currency, RMB is more than often an investment currency. When expectation on RMB appreciation is strong, investors who hold dim sum bonds can obtain not only interest income but also the potential benefit of appreciation. When expectation on RMB depreciation prevails, investors who hold dim sum bonds will require higher interest income to make up for the potential exchange rate loss in the future. Hence, the interest rate of dim sum bonds will rise with the depreciation expectation.

Liquidity in China's monetary market was quite tight in

2013 and many enterprises inclined to issue dim sum bonds in the offshore market. Because of RMB appreciation expectation at that time and relatively higher domestic interest rates, these enterprises were enthusiastic about issuance of dim sum bonds. But as RMB depreciation expectation prevails and domestic short-term interest rates remain low, onshore and offshore RMB interest rates have gradually converged and domestic enterprises lost their interest in bond issuance in Hong Kong. The issuance of dim sum bonds in 2016 was only 46.9 billion yuan, down by 50%. If RMB depreciation expectation persists, the market of dim sum bonds will continue to shrink.

RMB internationalization has entered a new development phase. In a long-term view, China's huge economic development potential and room for market-oriented reforms as well as the need of a diversified monetary system to support global financial stability would be the fundamental driving forces behind RMB internationalization. However, in the short term, RMB internationalization faces many challenges and needs to adjust its development mode. If market players using and holding RMB is determined by if they can obtain benefit or lower risk. The recent trend of market change keeps reducing the marginal benefit of holding RMB. On the one hand, there is limited room for RMB appreciation in the short term as China's economic growth is slowing down, import and export becomes balanced, and RMB exchange rate has basically reached an equilibrium level. On the other hand, there is an about-turn in global liquidity and RMB liquidity and the divergence between China's monetary policy and the US monetary policy will widen in the future. As a result, the narrowed interest rate gap between China and the US and the rise of US dollar will keep reducing the attraction of RMB. Moreover, since processing trade still accounts for a large share of China's trade and domestic exporters generally don't have much pricing power, it is difficult to increase the ratio of RMB-denominated trade. In terms of channels for capital flow, official development aids or investments may, to a certain extent, unleash RMB liquidity. But domestic financial institutions' lack of international competitiveness and experience in managing exchange risks has limited their role in promoting RMB internationalization. All evidences show that RMB internationalization has entered a new phase of stable development. China needs to gradually upgrade industrial and trade structure of its real economy in the future to raise the potential of RMB internationalization. Also, during the course to realize full convertibility of capital account, China needs to maintain ample prudential regulatory tools to prevent cross-border capital from promoting RMB internationalization with financial bubbles.

3 Cooperation Strategy for BRICS to Promote Internationalization of their Currencies

1. Promote Development of Bond Markets of Local Currencies

BRICS have relied heavily on banks (such as China and Russia) or international capital (such as India and Brazil) for boosting economic growth while the bond markets of their local currencies are all less developed. Though China and Russia boast huge foreign exchange reserves, most of such reserves are invested in the bond markets of western developed countries. These factors have led to currency and maturity mismatching in the financial systems of BRICS. If efforts can be made to develop the bond markets of their local currencies and enhance the investment and financing functions of these markets, BRICS will to a large extent reduce their excessive dependence not only on banks or international capital for financing but also on dollar assets for outbound financial investment.

The bond markets of local currencies are the main place to lower financial risks and boost long-term capital formation. Since the bond market is usually related to fixed-income products, low volatility, qualified institutional investors and block trade, it makes an ideal open transaction platform for investors with high risk aversion. As a fundamental market, the bond market can bring into full play its advantage as an opening-up channel in fund-raising and investment. In terms of the structure of products and investors, there is still ample room for development of the bond markets of BRICS currencies.

The importance of developing bonds markets of local currencies is even more obvious given BRICS' need to promote internationalization of their currencies. As above mentioned, one of the key symbols of currency internationalization is that this currency has become an international reserve currency. Most international reserves will be kept not in the form of cash but in the form of bonds denominated with this currency (usually including government bonds as well as a few large-cap financial bonds and corporate bonds). Therefore, their currency can possibly become an international reserve currency only after the development of bond markets with BRICS local currencies has made huge progress. In this sense, development of their local currency bond markets is one of the important steps to help BRICS realize currency internationalization.

(1) Establishment of a credit-enhancing and guarantee mechanism

For investors, the attraction of local-currency bond markets is determined by multiple factors including the risk and yield of bonds they issued, the size and liquidity level of the bond market, the financial openness of the currency-issuing country, the degree of internationalization of the denomination currency and its exchange rate expectation and so on. Among them, the risk and yield of bonds is an elemental factor. In this regard, credit rating agencies' rating over the fund-raiser will directly decide not only if the bond issuance will succeed but also the cost of financing. Hence, it is crucial to the development of local-currency bond markets for BRICS countries to establish a guarantee mechanism of bond credit enhancement to raise credit ratings for their government and corporate bonds. Generally speaking, the credit grade of bonds is determined by the higher one between the issuer and the guarantor. When the bond issuer and the external guarantor are completely independent from each other, their cooperation will substantially improve their joint debt-paying ability to lower default risk and issuance cost. [1]We think efforts should be strengthened in two aspects for establishing a guarantee mechanism. First, the New Development Bank (BRICS bank) should provide guarantee for local-currency bond issuance. Second, a BRICS guarantee fund should be set up to provide credit enhancement for local-currency bond issuance.

First, the New Development Bank can make use of its high credit rating to provide guarantee service for local-currency bond issuance. In this regard, the experience of European Investment Bank (EIB) and its subsidiary European Investment Fund (EIF) is worth learning. Through a number of traditional guarantee tools, EIB and EIF have supported financing by small and medium-sized European enterprises including start-ups, innovative small and medium-

---

[1] According to the author's statistic, the average issuance interest rate of domestic real estate enterprises that have gnarantee is 316bp lower than that without guarantee.

sized enterprises (SMEs) and other SMEs meeting specific program requirements. And the business scope of their guarantee (counter guarantee) covers loans, financial leasing and bond issuance. Besides, in the emerging business of asset securitization, EIF has attached great importance to innovation of guarantee tools. It helped issuers of securitization products to diversify sources of funds by providing guarantee for them. And it also helped lower economic cost and regulatory cost by means of credit risk transfer. In recent years, EIB and EIF have become the leader of credit enhancement for European SMEs. Their status as a multilateral development bank and their AAA grade had enabled financial institutions in cooperation to apply a zero risk weight to assets under their guarantee. In 2015 alone, EIF had obtained a net income of 49.561 million euro from guarantee business.

Second, a BRICS credit guarantee fund can be set up to provide guarantee for local-currency bond issuance. In addition to the above-mentioned EIF, the experience of the Credit Guarantee Association in Japan in providing guarantee to facilitate financing and bond transaction by Japanese enterprises is also worth learning. In 2004, Japan announced the establishment of "Asian Bond Insurance Mechanism" to provide guarantee for issuance of foreign bonds by Japanese enterprises investing in East Asian countries, helping them raise funds in the destination country of investment. This measure has opened a new path for Japanese enterprises to raise funds through bond issuance in East Asian countries. A guarantee fund co-funded by BRICS countries can surely assume a similar role as the Credit Guarantee Association in Japan has done. And this fund can be set up under the New Development Bank so they can operate in the model of EIB and EIF.

(2) Strengthen interbank market cooperation among BRICS

Construction of the interbank market is central to the development of one country's bond market. Currently, the bond markets of BRICS are still severely separated from each other not only because of the stark difference among their rules and regulations, credit ratings, accounting risk audit and settlement system for transaction and clearing but also the different degrees of maturity of their bond markets. The connectivity construction among the bond markets of BRICS has not made a breakthrough while their bond issuance and transaction volume are rising. The structure of investors, most of which, are commercial banks and insurance companies, has led to the predominance of safe asset in the market transaction, limiting free flow of market capital and weakening the bond market's function of financing and fund-raising. It is our suggestion that BRICS should strengthen interbank market cooperation through following measures: setting up an efficient BRICS cross-border clearing settlement system; improving compatibility among their accounting and auditing standards as well as related laws and regulations through consultation; relaxing requirements on access for investors among themselves to diversify the structure of investors and allow complementary cooperation among BRICS investors in the aspects of capital, information and technology. Implementation of these measures will help investors realize diversified investment returns in the BRICS interbank markets and reduce investment risks, effectively increase transactions and turnover rate to facilitate reasonable flow of capital and promote stable development of interbank markets in BRICS countries.

2. Boost (cross-border) Investment and Financing with BRICS Currencies

There are several models to boost (cross-border) investment and financing with BRICS currencies: the first is that overseas financial institutions will raise funds with local currency in one BRICS country for their overseas investment (mainly in another BRICS country); the second is that domestic financial institutions from one BRICS country will raise funds with local currency for their overseas investment (mainly in another BRICS country); the third is that overseas financial institutions will raise fund in one BRICS country with the currency of another BRICS country for their overseas investment as Table 9 shows. In addition to the above-mentioned three models, three other models can be developed that fund-raising financial institutions will not invest in one country but invest through providing credit financing. So, there can be six models to boost (cross-border) investment and financing with BRICS currencies.

Table 9   **Models for cross-border investment and financing with**

BRICS currencies

	Financing institution	Financing country	Currency	Investment destination
Mode 1	Financial institutions beyond BRICS country A	BRICS country A	Currency of BRICS country A	Investment in BRICS countries except A
Mode 2	Financial institutions from BRICS country A	BRICS country A	Currency of BRICS country A	Investment in BRICS countries except A

(contd.)

	Financing institution	Financing country	Currency	Investment destination
Mode3	Financial institutions beyond BRICS country A	BRICS countries except A	Currency of BRICS country A	Investment in BRICS countries (including A)

According to the above models, we make following suggestions to boost (cross-border) investment and financing with BRICS currencies:

First, financial institutions should be encouraged to raise funds from one BRICS country with local currency and then use them to invest in another BRICS country. For instance, the New Development Bank can issue RMB-denominated bonds in China and then use the fund raised to invest in BRICS countries. International development institutions like the International Finance Corporation under the United Nations and Asian Development Bank had issued RMB bonds (Panda Bond) in China's interbank bond market in 2005 and 2013 respectively for investment in China. In consideration of RMB internationalization, the "going-out" of Chinese enterprises and China's advantage in infrastructural construction, it is fully workable to invest in other BRICS countries with RMB.

Second, related institutions of BRICS countries should

be encouraged to raise funds in local currencies of other BRICS countries and then use them for domestic investment or providing credit support. For instance, Russia's ministry of finance decided to issue offshore RMB bonds in Russia in December 2016. Therefore, the issuance of RMB bonds by commercial banks or other non-financial institutions in other BRICS countries will provide them with more sources for financing.

Third, the BRICS countries should set up investment funds with local currencies based on the New Development Bank. These funds will be operated by the New Development Bank, and their investment direction and business mode will be designed according to the actual demand of each BRICS country. For example, they can set up infrastructure investment fund and climate change investment fund. There can be multiple financing sources for these funds. For instance, they can issue local currency bonds in the five countries so as to support the development of the local currency bond markets of BRICS countries.

3. Further Promote Currency Swap and Direct Trading with Local Currency

Though BRICS countries have established a Contingent

Reserve Arrangement, this arrangement aims to maintain financial stability by providing short-term liquidity support when member countries face international payment pressure. Meanwhile, the currency swap under this arrangement is one between US dollar and local currencies of BRICS, not one among BRICS currencies. Currently, China has signed currency swap agreements with Brazil (expired), Russia and South Africa. In future, a currency swap network among local currencies of BRICS countries should be improved. For China, it should restart currency swap with Brazil as early as possible while actively explore the possibility of currency swap with India. For other BRICS countries, they should also actively explore the possibility of setting up bilateral currency swap among themselves. Among all BRICS currencies, RMB has already developed direct trading with Russian Rouble and South Africa Rand. Direct trading between RMB and other BRICS currencies should be built in the future.

4. Promote Local-currency Settlement in Commodity Trading

The extreme instability of the present global political

and economic environment has led to volatile fluctuations in the prices of commodities. Because most commodities are priced in US dollar in the international market, including oil, natural gas, iron ore, copper, nickel and grain, enterprises from BRICS countries can only passively accept the volatile price fluctuation, adding to the risk for their production and operation. In face of this reality, BRICS countries should realize local currency settlement in commodity trading as soon as possible to increase their pricing power in global commodity trade and promote diversification of settlement currencies in commodity trade, which is of vital importance to stabilize manufacturing prices and reducing cost in BRICS countries. If the international trade of energy, minerals, grains and commodities closely related to people's life are priced in local currencies, BRICS countries will be able to not only avoid the impact of foreign exchange fluctuation on their domestic inflation but also reduce transaction cost for enterprises resulting from buying or selling foreign exchange and living cost for residents who will consume those commodities. Meanwhile, realization of local currency settlement in commodity trading among BRICS countries will, in fact, contribute to the diversification of the international monetary system. One key measurement of the diversification of the international monetary system is the diversification of settlement currencies in international commodity trade.

Among BRICS countries, China and India are all major importers of raw materials while Russia and Brazil are major exporters of raw materials. This fact will help connect supply and demand among BRICS countries and facilitate local currency settlement in commodity trade among BRICS countries. BRICS countries' resources endowment and huge potential for economic development have decided that they will play a central role in the reform to diversify settlement currencies in international commodity trade. They should make full use of this advantage to improve top-down design and promote local-currency commodity trade through multiple means.

First, BRICS countries should accelerate construction of the platform for international commodity trade, setting up a multi-layer commodity market system that includes spot, OTC and futures markets and is open to both domestic and overseas investors, in particular, improving market functions for spot, futures, options, forwards and swap transactions.

Second, international application of local-currency-denominated commodities should be expanded. Specifically speaking, BRICS countries should expedite construction of international exchanges and propel their domestic futures exchanges and spot exchanges to accelerate internationalization of transactions of local-currency-denominated commodities contracts on iron ores and palm oil, attract more overseas investors and increase transaction volume. In addition, they can also develop financial products denominated with local currencies in carbon trade in view of their own actual carbon emission.

Finally, complementary financial service for commodity trade should also be improved. Specifically speaking, one is to set up a BRICS payment system for cross-border settlement. Another one is to enhance BRICS commercial banks' financial innovation in commodities. For instance, they can deepen cooperation with commodity futures exchanges, spot trading platforms, OTC derivatives markets, provide local-currency-denominated subject matter of commodities to both domestic and overseas investors, and provide dealers with comprehensive financial service including account, foreign exchange, settlement, financing, wealth management, brokerage and consultation. The third one is to propel the "New Development Bank" to provide trade financing in

BRICS currencies and design related local-currency-denominated hedging tools to raise the pricing power of BRICS currencies in commodity trading and provide enterprises with risk management tools needed in settlement of commodity trading.

5. Promote Cross-border Financial Infrastructural Construction in BRICS Countries with Blockchain Technology

This report believes that establishing the BRICS cross-border interbank payment system on the basis of blockchain technology might be a key step of BRICS cross-border financial infrastructural construction because it will not only significantly improve the efficiency of cross-border interbank payment among BRICS countries but also exert a fundamental impact on the international monetary and financial system.

In the current international monetary system, the US dollar plays a dominant role in cross-border payment and settlement. The dollar payment and settlement of international trade is mainly carried out through " Society for Worldwide Interbank Financial Telecommunications "

(SWIFT) and "Clearing House Interbank Payment System" (CHIPS). SWIFT, as the nerve center of the global banking industry, has maintained close business in 210 countries and regions around the world while providing interbank transactions and financial information exchange to more than 10,000 banks and financial institutions everyday, with as much as 6 trillion dollar involved.

Blockchain technology may fundamentally change the current international payment and settlement system. In essence, blockchain is a huge decentralized distributed ledger database. As a P2P network based on open-source software and structure, blockchain has many characteristics such as decentralization, no need of a trusted authority, disintermediation, inherent resistant to modification and safe encryption in the currency-related fields such as transaction payment in comparison with the support of traditional network. The characteristics of blockchain will change the "center-periphery" operational model of the traditional financial system: in terms of financial institutions, central banks are the center and commercial banks are the periphery; in terms of cross-border payment and settlement platform, SWIFT and CHIPS are the center and other systems are the periphery. Because blockchain is safe, transparent, distributed and tamper resistant, the trust model between financial systems will no longer rely on intermediation and many banks will make their businesses "decentralized" and realize real-time digital transactions.

Though blockchain technology is not mature, all sides believe that there is huge room for applying blockchain in cross-border payment settlement. The current cross-border payment and settlement not only is time-consuming and costly but also involves many intermediary links. Blockchain can realize fast, cheap and point-to-point cross-border payment without the use of an intermediary bank. The blockchain platform can not only bypass the intermediary bank to save intermediary fees but also improve safety of cross-border remittances and speed up clearing and settlement to increase utilization rate of funds because of its characteristics of safety, transparency and low risk. In the future, banks will not need a third party but use blockchain technology to realize point-to-point payment. The removal of the intermediary link of the third-party financial institution means cross-border payment will no longer depend on systems such as SWIFT and CHIPS.

The characteristic of decentralization of blockchain technology has enabled payment without involving a third-party institution. Such a technology has overthrown the dependence of the traditional financial system on the center, lowering the cost to build "credit" around the globe. In the international monetary system under the dominance of the US dollar, the credibility of the US dollar as international currency originates from the strength of the US economy. Other countries' trust in the US dollar system has led to their adoption of the US dollar as the medium for payment and clearing. Since blockchain is safe, transparent and tamper resistant, the trust model among financial systems will no longer rely on intermediation. And this will fundamentally shake the predominance of the US dollar in international payment settlement.

Overseas institutions have already realized the importance of blockchain to cross-border payment and settlement. Currently, except the "utility settlement coin" put forward by UBS, Ripple, a US company, is the first Fintech company to carry out cross-border settlement based on blockchain concept. Banks from 17 countries have cooperated with the company to realize point-to-point cross-border interbank transfer via the company's network. Meanwhile, SWIFT is trying to develop its own distributed ledger platform, exploring how to integrate distributed ledger into its payment system and have itself thorough overhauled with blockchain technology.

Due to inadequate regulation over blockchain, financial institutions from BRICS have not participated deeply in blockchain cross-border payment and settlement. But in view of the possible huge impact blockchain technology may exert on the international payment and settlement system, BRICS countries should promote establishment an cross-border payment and settlement system based on blockchain technology among themselves so as to take an advantageous position in the reform of the international monetary and financial system.

First, BRICS should continue to follow the latest progress of the development of blockchain technology and gradually expand application of blockchain technology. According the view of Melanie Swan, founder of Institute for Blockchain Studies, The changes that blockchain technology has brought about and will bring about can be divided into three categories: Blockchain 1.0, Blockchain 2.0 and Blockchain 3.0. Blockchain 1.0 refers to digital currency and its applications are about currency, including currency transfer, foreign exchange and payment system. Blockchain 2.0 refers to smart contract and its applications are mainly in economic, market and financial sectors but can be extended to a scope much broader than simple cash transfer, including stocks, bonds, futures, loans, mortgage, property rights and smart contract. Blockchain 3.0 refers to applications beyond currency, finance and market which mainly concerns government, health, science, culture and art. BRICS countries' understanding of blockchain is still at the first level of digital currency. In the future, BRICS countries should gradually encourage application of blockchain technology in the financial sector and strengthen cooperation and coordination among their blockchain institutions.

Second, BRICS should participate in discussing regulation over blockchain in international cross-border payment and settlement and drafting industry standards. BRICS countries' monetary authorities and financial institutions should pool their values and claims and jointly develop industry standards to guide international regulation and draw new rules for the financial system. Today, the application of blockchain by the global banking industry is still in the initial phase of development, facing a series of choices over technologies and models as well as various possibilities regarding regulatory compliance and application scope. Three forces including blockchain Fintech companies, large banks and regulators will largely determine the direction and standards for blockchain applications by banks in the future, and regulators will become a leading force for applications of blockchain technology. If BRICS countries have implemented blockchain cooperation among themselves, they will assume a bigger role in the future when taking part in negotiation of related international rules. Through consultation among their regulators, BRICS countries can set up industry regulation and related technological standards and make rules for the game to seize market opportunities.

Finally, BRICS countries should set up a blockchain cooperation platform and encourage cooperation between financial institutions and Fintech companies to establish a BRICS cross-border payment system based on blockchain as soon as possible. Though the United States and Europe have set up blockchain-based cross-border payment companies, their internal technological application remains unsatisfactory. For instance, XRP issued by Ripple face big troubles in circulation as 30% of them are held by the founder and charities. Blockchain cross-border payment technology is still in the early stage of development. It may take years or more than a decade for such a technology to be widely applied. At present, BRICS countries can set up blockchain cooperation platforms, organize financial institutions to establish blockchain labs and cooperate with Fintech companies to develop technologies that can be applied in core businesses, and set up common industry standards. On the one hand, they should set up a BRICS cross-border interbank payment system step by step. On the other hand, they should actively participate in making the global industry standards.

References

BIS (2015), "Digital Currency", Committee on Payments and Market Infrastructures of BIS, http://www. bis. org/cpmi/publ/d137. pdf.

Christine Lagarde (2017), "Fintech—A Brave New World for the Financial Sector?", IMF Blog, https://blogs. imf. org/2017/03/21/fintech-a-brave-new-world-for-the-financial-sector/.

Dong He, Karl Habermeier, etc. (2016), "Virtual Currencies and Beyond: Initial Considerations", IMF Staff Discussion Note, http://www. imf. org/external/pubs/ft/sdn/2016/sdn1603. pdf.

Gao H. and Yu Y. (2012), "Internationalization of the Renminbi", Bank for International Settlements, BIS paper No. 61, pp. 105 – 24, http://www. bis. org/repoffi-cepubl/arpresearch200903. 05. pdf.

Javier Sebastian Cermeno(2016) , "Blockchain in Financial Services: Regulatory Landscape and Future Challenges for its Commercial Application" , Working Paper, BBVA Research, https://www. bbvaresearch. com/wp-content/uploads/2016/12/WP_16-20. pdf.

Joseph S. Nye (2013) , "BRICS without Mortar" , Project Syndicate, April 3, https://www. project-syndicate. org/commentary/why-brics-will-not-work-by-joseph-s--nye? barrier = accessreg.

Liu D. (2016) , "Internationalization of China's Bonds Markets, Development of Offshore RMB Center and Provision of Global Safe Assets" , in *Enter the Dragon: China in the International Financial System*, CIGI Press.

Liu D. (2016) , "Offshore issuance of China's Local Government Bond" , *Zhongguo Jinrong* (China Finance) , No. 17, pp. 76 – 77.

Liu D. , Gao H. , Xu Q. , Li Y. and Song S. (2017) , "China's Next Steps in Renminbi Internationalization: The Renminbi as a Reserve Asset and an Investment Vehicle, the 'Belt and Road' Initiative and the Role of London" , Chatham House.

Song S. , Liu D. (2016) , "The EIB's Non-Credit Business for Small and Medium Enterprises and Its Implication for the AIIB", *Yinhangjia* (The Chinese Bankers), No. 10, pp:108 – 111.

Thorsten K and Jeremy K (2017), "Blockchain Technology—What's in Store for Canada's Economy and Financial Markets?", https://www. cdhowe. org/public-policy-research/blockchain-technology-% E2% 80% 93-what% E2% 80% 99s-store-canada% E2% 80% 99s-economy-and-financial-markets.

WEF (2016), " The Future of Financial Infrastructure", An Industry Project of the Financial Services Community, the World Economic Forum, http://www3. weforum. org/docs/WEF_The_future_of_financial_infrastructure. pdf.

Wu Y. (2013), "Analysis of the Currency Swap Approach of the RMB Internationalization", *Shanghai Jinrong* (*Shanghai Finance*), No. 4, pp. 32 – 36.

Liu Dongmin is a senior research fellow and the director of Division of International Finance, Institute of World Economics and Politics, Chinese Academy of Social Sciences. He graduated from Tsinghua University, getting a Bachelor's Degree of Engineering and Master's Degree of Management Science and Engineering. After that, he got a Ph. D of Finance in the Chinese Academy of Social Sciences. Now he is an adviser of the Ministry of Finance for the AIIB affairs. His research area focuses on reform of international monetary system, internationalization of RMB, development of the AIIB and BRICs Bank, bond market, etc. He has deeply participated in the Financial Industry Planning for Qianhai Free Trade Zone in Guangdong Province, and three of his proposals were approved by the central government in 2012. Up to now his proposal of cross-border RMB loan has already successfully applied to China's FTZs (Shanghai City, Tianjin City, Guangdong Province and Fujian Province) and over RMB 100 billion of cross-border RMB loans have been issued.

Xiao Lisheng, deputy director, senior research fellow and master student advisor of International Finance Research Division, Institute of World Economics and Politics, Chinese Academy of Social Sciences. His main research fields are China's macro economy and international finance. He has published several papers on authoritative journals, such as *Economic Research* (Chinese) , *Management World* , and *Journal of Financial Research* (Chinese). He participated in national and ministerial level of macroeconomic seminars, and wrote number of decision-making advisory reports and won the Excellent Countermeasure Information Award from the Chinese Academy of Social Sciences (Countermeasure Research Category). He also serves as an external master student advisor of the University of International Business and Economics, and a consultant to the Ministry of Finance's International Economic Relations Division and a researcher at the Pangu think tank、China Finance 40 Youth Forum and the International political and financial security think tank.

Lu Ting, Ph. D in economics, Associate research fellow at the Institute of World Economy and Politics, used to conduct her post-doctoral study at the People's bank of China. The research interests are international finance, financial stabilities and asset pricing.

Xiong Aizong is an assistant research fellow in Institute of World Economics and Politics (IWEP) , Chinese Academy of Social Science (CASS). He has studied Economics at Xiamen University and obtained a Ph. D in Economics (2010). Dr. XIONG was as an assistant professor in School of Economics, Xiamen University from 2010 to 2011, and did two-year postdoctoral research at Institute of International Economics in Nankai University from 2011 to 2013. His research areas include global economic governance and international money and finance, and now his research interests also include issues of emerging market economies, especially BRICS countries.

Zhang Chi is a post doctor of Division of International Finance, Institute of World Economics and Politics, Chinese Academy of Social Sciences. She graduated from Nankai University with a Ph. D in economics. She published several academic papers in China's economics journals, and she also joined several research programs invited by different ministries of Chinese central government. Her interests mainly focus on international finance, including bond market, international capital flow and RMB internationalization.

This book is the result of a co-publication agreement between China Social Sciences Press (China) and Paths International Ltd (UK)

Title: The Internationalization of BRICS Currencies: China's Experiences and Cooperation Strategy
Author: Liu Dongmin, Xiao Lisheng, Lu Ting, Xiong Aizong, Zhang Chi
ISBN: 978-1-84464-559-6
Ebook ISBN: 978-1-84464-560-2

Paths International Ltd
www.pathsinternational.com
Published in the United Kingdom

CPSIA information can be obtained
at www.ICGtesting.com
Printed in the USA
LVHW020334070121
675928LV00003B/5